From The Heart

Erica Wakefield

BookLeaf Publishing

India | USA | UK

Presentation by *BookLeaf Publishing*

Web: www.bookleafpub.com

E-mail: info@bookleafpub.com

ISBN: 9789358315035

First edition 2024

DEDICATION

I dedicate this to book to anyone who needs the opportunity to laugh, cry, get angry or process weird thoughts of their own. May reading this book give you that space.

ACKNOWLEDGEMENT

I owe a lot of my inspiration to those who have
supported my life's journey:
Parents, Lovers, Friends, Family, Pets
And those who have caused me pain - you've
helped to make me stronger than you ever will
be, so thanks.

PREFACE

I've always seen poetry as a way of expressing what I hold inside. For some reason, a poem can say things better than talking to someone face to face.

I have faced many challenges in life, accomplished many goals and learned a lot: something these poems reflect.

The Long Walk

A young woman walks along the canal
Haunted by a pain she knows only too well
Her heart is heavy, her footsteps slow
Her face looks white in the pale moon glow
She stops for a while and sinks to her knees
Her tear stained cheeks cooled by the breeze
A white rose is laid to show innocence lost:
Being together came with such a high cost
Next to the white rose is one of deep red:
A symbol of blood that had cruelly been shed
She lights a small candle, pain growing inside
Her mind going back to the day that he died
As the darkness of night is replaced by the day
She dries her tears before walking away
Her heart is heavy as she says her goodbyes
Her hope, like the candle flame, flickers and
dies.

A Heathen Heart

You think you know our Heathen history?
Probably not – we are a mystery

Mind you, you got some parts right:
Like drinking and boasting by pale moonlight

With beards and shouting we look quite scary
But we're friendly folks (though some are hairy)

We celebrate the Gods of old
We honour those who now lay cold

We offer food, drink and heat
To the eager, curious folks we meet

We are not evil, we do not kill
Or drag in new members against their will

The path we walk is sometimes tough
But we support each other when things are
rough

So do not judge us or criticise
Or look at us with hateful eyes

Our ways may differ to your own
But we too are all but flesh and bone

We welcome questions from those unsure
We teach with compassion at our core

So do not judge what you dont understand
We've as much right as you to walk this land.

Stuck In The Teacup

A woman got stuck in the Teacup ride.
She began to shout
"You stupid cow, stop the ride.
I'm stuck. I can't get out!"

In my years of operating rides
Noone had been stuck before
I thought "If I dont do something
I'll lose my job for sure"

I walked over to the teacup
To see what I could do.
I said "It's ok. Im here to help.
I'll take good care of you".

Her face turned a beetroot red
She wriggled about in the seat
Out of her mouth came words
Too vulgar to repeat!

The management took her away
With help from the security team
I sat there in the ride cabin
Trying not to scream.

The rest of the shift seemed ok
Apart from the pain in my head
I knew the next day was my day off
I intended to spend it in bed!

So if you can pinch
Much more than an inch
And your backside is too big to fit
Remember the moral of my true tale:
If the Teacup's too small, don't ride it!!

Progress

As the last blade of grass is torn out
As the last tree is cut down
As the last white cloud becomes black with
toxins
I hear an old man whisper:
"Its the devil, progress"

Concrete replaces nature
Raw waste replaces fresh water
Wild animals' homes are replaced by the human
kind
All in the name of:
The devil, progress.

A young child asks what a tree looks like
As he searches through the rubble
A building site now his playground
He's lost his innocence
To thy devil...progress.

Weight Watchers

Our Weight Watchers Club
Who art in Alsager Civic Centre (Tuesdays
5-8pm).

Hated be thy weigh-ins.

Thy boring diet and impossible exercise plan
shall be done
At home, as it is in the meetings.

Give us this day our daily celery stick
And forgive us our nibble of a cream cake
As we forgive the bakers who made them in the
first place.

Lead us not into temptation
But deliver us from anything with more than 2g
of fat in it.

For mine are the fruit, the salad and the water
Forever and ever (or til I can fit into my size 10
skirt)
Amen

Another Statistic

For years you've treated me like dirt
With kicks, punches and words that hurt.
Bruises, grazes and a broken heart
A life that feels like its falling apart.
An arm in a sling, a body battered.
My self-worth gone, confidence shattered.
A daily life of constant pain
Of feeling trapped, again and again.
I feel like an animal caught in a snare
No one to love it, no one to care.
There's no escape, no way out
No one to hear me scream or shout.
I'm sworn to secrecy, kept in silence
Another statistic of domestic violence.

Freshers Week

New sights, new sounds.
Nervous people all around.
Anxiety soars, hearts race.
Sweaty palms, pale face.
Meet new people, dont be shy.
Trying so hard not to cry.
First night, get drunk.
Flirt with any handsome hunk.
Early morning, most in bed.
Lie awake with throbbing head.
Later on, all seems ok
New friends, bright new day.

Typical Bloke

He sits there watching football on his wide
screen colour TV.
An outsider couldn't fail to notice, it gets more
attention than me!
I have to check his breathing to make sure he's
still alive.
I'll say "Hey big boy, come up to bed" but no
chance: it's the FA cup live.
While he was at work one day, I thought "I'll
give him a surprise.
I'll wear my kinky maids outfit - he won't
believe his eyes!
Maybe I'll go for full leathers with a bullwhip in
one hand
I'll say "Don't call me darling: it's mistress to
you. Understand?"
I thought a bit of foreplay could ignite a much
needed spark.
I thought we could give a new meaning to things
going bump in the dark
I took hours to get everything ready so that when
he walked through the door
he'd see my bra with a note which reads "Leave
all your clothes on the floor"

The front door slammed shut and I thought "here
we go!
I hope he's got stamina - I'm not taking it slow"
But my ears heard a sound that they heard every
day since we married in '83.
I thought "surely not. Not again. What a waste!
He's watching bloody football on TV!"

Last Dance

Nameless figures, dressed in black, walk past me
as I stare
Half-hidden in the darkness, away from the
street lamp glare.
Crosses, ankhs and pentagrams: such trinkets
they all don -
Yet most will leave their necks exposed for me
to gaze upon.
I wrap my coat around me as I blend into the
crowd
Lost in a world of flashing lights and music
played too loud.
I search the mass of faces for one I knew before
-
She promised she would wait for me but I am
not so sure.
Finally I see her, my heart now beating fast.
I fight my way through bodies, ignoring those I
pass.
Her eyes shine with recognition- grateful for the
chance
To have me hold her in my arms and embrace
her when we dance.
I long to make this moment last but time is not
my friend.

Being with her forever would mean her life must
end.
How can I make her what I am? Can I watch that
final breath -
That sends her to her sleep alive then wakes her
up in death?
I know I must carry on alone and she, for now,
must stay
So I kiss her softly, dry her tears then turn and
drift away.

Blank Page

I sit, staring at the blank page.
Blank, just like my mind.
Eyes cold and heavy.
I hear people scribbling away.
I just sit there, staring.
Then I get a thought.
A flow of words and emotions.
Washing around my brain like an ocean.
Yet my hands won't write.
They feel like they are stuck.
Unable or unwilling to move.
The words flow and people scribble.
So many distractions!
More words come: harsh, angry
In need of writing down.
Emotions: hate, love, passion, confusion
Im frustrated.
So much to write
Yet the page stays blank.
Too many words...
Not enough time.
Drowning in an ocean
Of thoughts and emotion.

Face In The Mirror

I look in the mirror but don't like what I see:
The fragile young woman staring at me.
Her uncombed hair frames her pale face.
Her sighing chest covered in torn, black lace.
She looks so empty, she feels so cold
Like a lump of clay awaiting its mould.
Her bright, pretty eyes now look sad and grey.
What did I do to make you this way?
As I walk away I hear her shout my name
Asking to swap places, saying I'm to blame.
I choose to break the mirror but even when its
smashed
I still can feel her watching me through broken
shards of glass.

One Night Romance

Your eyes met mine
On that cold, winter night.
When my hand met your thigh
You soon set that right!
Then came romance
I was all of a flutter.
When your lips met mine
My heart melted like butter.
My knees turned to jelly.
I broke out in a sweat.
That night on Asda carpark?
I will never forget.
We went back to my place
That's when you got
A bit too adventurous
You said "ooh I'm hot!"
So off came your clothes
While I stood there
You whipped off your tights
And the gold underwear.
I swallowed and gulped.
I felt a bit faint.
I thought "love may be blind
But the neighbours ain't!"
After the argy bargy

And bouncing about on the bed
You rolled over and went to sleep
"That was fantastic", I said.
The next day, you left me.
My heart felt like lead.
But then another girl came along.
"Such is life", I said!

Final Meeting

I remember the loving smile
You always used to share.
The way you touched my face
Or softly stroked my hair.
Now it's all gone.
My life moves on.
You use to bounce me gently
On your strong and sturdy knee.
We looked deep in each other's eyes
Our faces filled with glee.
Now it's all gone.
Life moves slowly on.
I still see you at my window
But then you disappear.
Whenever I am sad or scared
I know you will be near.
The background behind me is fading
As we move towards each other.
Goodbye friends and colleagues.
Goodbye father and mother.
We're now in peace and happy
Side by side, together.
Please do not weep for me.
I'll live on in your heart forever.
I've left the ones I love so much.

To them I can only say:
Don't stay sad for too long.
Im not that far away.

Fancy That

"Just fancy that", my parents say
To anything I mention.
They always seem so far away
They never pay attention.
"The parrot's been sick on the carpet.
The dog's chasing next doors cat.
The rabbit is chewing the table leg"
"Oh really?" they say "Fancy that!"
"In the bathroom, there's a spider.
In the kitchen, a giant rat.
In the garden, there's a unicorn"
"Oh really?" they say "Fancy that!"
So today I'm telling them
That I said naughty word.
The way the vicar hurried past
I'm positive he heard!
"You wicked, naughty boy" they shout.
"You horrid, little brat!"
At last I think they've noticed me.
My goodness, fancy that!

Beggar Woman

She wanders alone through the dark, stormy
night.
Her eyes lost their sparkle, her face deathly
white.
Noone will talk to her or help if she cries
There's a pain in her sadness and a tear in her
eyes.
The coat on her back doesnt keep out the chill.
She knows that the winter is ready to kill.
Her body grows weaker, her life falls apart.
There now is a stone where she once had a heart.
Noone will talk to her or help if she cries.
There's a pain in her sadness and a tear in her
eyes.
The hands of time turn and she lets out a sigh.
Alone she has travelled and alone she must die.
There's noone to help her as she struggles for
breath.
There's a pain in her sadness as she waits for her
death.

Valentine's Day

You're not as a sexy as you used to be when I
met you in 1954.
Your perfect size 10 figure is now more like size
24.
You used to have hair down to your waist that I
could play with in bed.
Now it's receded and the hair down below has
started to grow up instead.
Sex isn't as good as it was years ago, you've not
got the stamina any more.
But still, I know I shouldn't complain
considering you're 74!
I know that old age can affect the grey matter
and you sometimes forget people's names
Although your brainpower is all but extinct, I
love you just the same.
So on this Valentine's day, my love, we can
snuggle up together.
Moaning and whinging for another year about
love, life and the weather.

Shapes In Shadows

If you go down to the park at night
You may get a nasty surprise
A feeling that you're being watched
By cold, resentful eyes.
Waiting in the darkness
For a victim to pass by
The sound of evil laughter
Drowns out the anguished cry.
You're drained of all your energy
Left lying close to death
The only strength you have
Fades with every breath.
If only you had stayed in bed
With the covers pulled up tight
But like a lamb to slaughter
You ventured out tonight.
You've passed the point of no return
Too late for turning back
There's no chance of hope or rescue
When you leave the beaten track.
Don't let the shadows tempt you
To follow them, to play.
Don't mess with what you don't understand
Just turn and run away.

Last Chance

One last chance
One more dance
Too soon to say goodbye
One last chance
One more dance
Before the tears run dry

One night to hold you
One night to kiss
One night to be
With the one that I miss

One last chance
One more dance
Beneath the winter moon
One last chance
One more dance
Love taken away too soon

One night to hold you
One night to kiss
One night to be
With the one that I miss

One last chance

One more dance
Let you go? I must
One last chance
One final dance
Before you turn to dust.

Escape

Looking in the mirror, a woman starts to cry.
Trying to be brave as she whispers a goodbye.
Opening the bathroom door, she prays a silent prayer.
Hoping that her children wont find her body there.

Tablets like candy
Wait on the shelf
A way to escape
From being yourself

Thoughts of her kids are scorched on her mind.
How would they cope if she left them behind?
In guilt, she flushes each tablet away:
They can always be bought on another bad day.

Tablets like candy
Wait on the shelf
A way to escape
From being yourself.

Society

Where can you go?
What can you do
When society turns its back on you?

Ask the man who huddles against the wall of an
old, derelict shop forgotten by time.
The man who has sat by the same wall of the
same shop for as long as he can remember.
Or ask the woman who, when night falls,
scavanges in bins for a morsel of food.
Desperation clearly visible in her eyes if anyone
could be bothered to look.
Rejected by friends and family, ignored by
everyone else.
No one to help when the dark becomes darker
and the cold becomes colder.
Society tosses them out like ragdolls whose
owners have grown bored.

Where can you run to?
What do you do
When society is blind to what happens to you?

Ask the woman who huddles against the door in
a foetal position.

The woman who seems to have a habit of
walking into things (like a clenched fist).
Or ask the woman who lies face down on the
lounge carpet.
She watches the pattern her blood makes as it
dries.
She can't talk but she doesn't need to: the scars
are visible to people if they open their eyes.
Isolated, trapped, silently screaming to ears that
choose not to hear her.
Society pretends there is no problem,keeping it
locked behind closed doors (just like the
women).

Where can you hide?
What can you do
When religion tries to brainwash you?

Ask the child who sits silently, arms folded,
shoulders back, eyes facing forward.
The child whose parents believes that Satan lives
in their son or daughter and must be thrashed out
of them with bible and belt.
Or ask the thousands of men, women and
children whose blood runs like wine.
Those who dared to have an opinion different to
the ever contradictory religion that happens to be
in power.

Innocent people who wrongly believed that the
"freedom of religious expression" applied to
them as well.
You can ask, but dont expect a reply.
Its difficult having a conversation with a corpse.
Society justifies and encourages the mass
slaughter because "God wants us to do it".

Where can you go?
What can you do
In a society that destructively oppresses you?

Technology

Why are things so complicated?
Why can my brain not cope?
I've tried to keep up with technology
But I haven't got a hope.

I brought a new toaster the other week
But its driving me up the wall:
It throws the bread out at breakneck speed
Or sometimes wont pop up at all.

The laptop? Well, that's even worse
Many swear words have escaped my lips
I've tried to learn the computer lingo:
I know cookies and microchips!

It used to be easy when I was a lass
I could manage schoolwork just fine
Now the calculators kids are using
Could a frazzle an old head like mine.

My husband, he loves his satnav
But with me it always fails.
It keeps saying something about ewe turns
I guess it still thinks we're in Wales!

So keep your techno gadgets
Use them to your heart's desire
I'm going to sit back with wine and a book
And put more Kindles on the fire.

www.ingramcontent.com/pod-product-compliance
Lightning Source LLC
La Vergne TN
LVHW010934200726